I0415768

TRAINING AND READINESS MANUAL GROUP (TRMGI) CHARTER TERMS OF REFERENCE

DEPARTMENT OF THE NAVY
HEADQUARTERS UNITED STATES MARINE CORPS
3000 MARINE CORPS PENTAGON
WASHINGTON, D.C. 20350-3000

NAVMC 3500.106
C 469
7 Jul 2011

NAVMC 3500.106

From: Commandant of the Marine Corps
To: Distribution List

Subj: TRAINING AND READINESS MANUAL GROUP (TRMG) CHARTER TERMS OF REFERENCE

Ref: (a) MCO P3500.72A
      (b) MCO 3500.110
      (c) MCO 1200.13F

Encl: (1) Specific TRMG Guidance

1. <u>Purpose</u>. The Marine Corps Ground Training and Readiness (T&R) Program has been in existence since 1995. Recently, in an effort to improve the systematic process of developing and reviewing core training standards in support of approved Mission Essential Tasks (METs), the requirement to establish a Ground TRMG Charter Terms of Reference has been identified. This document is intended to provide an interim set of "business rules" governing the conduct of Ground Training and Readiness Manual review, revision and update until an overarching Marine Air Ground Task Force (MAGTF) T&R Program is established. References (a) through (c) apply.

   a. Effective immediately, Commanding General (CG), Training and Education Command (TECOM) establishes and manages the Ground TRMG terms of reference, identifying representation, roles and responsibilities for all vested stake holders and agencies within the Marine Corps who have a responsibility and interest in the systematic development, validation, improvement and maintenance of their respective T&R Manuals. Reference (a) details the overarching policy for the Marine Corps Ground T&R Program.

   b. This Manual defines TRMG Charter Terms of Reference in support of the Ground T&R Program, emphasizing continuity of subject matter expertise (SME) and member roles and responsibilities.

   c. Each TRMG charter forms the nucleus of specific T&R Manual development, validation and revision. TRMGs will develop, review, validate and revise individual and collective training standards (T&R Manuals) that align with and support current approved core METs. The Ground T&R Program serves as the cornerstone of providing commanders in the operating forces, supporting establishment and formal schools with the core standards required to plan and implement progressive training that ensures individual and collective training readiness within the current operational environment.

   d. A formalized process incorporated into a published Battle Rhythm that produces improved, contemporary service standards which further enable and assess MET training and readiness.

DISTRIBUTION STATEMENT A: Approved for public release; distribution is unlimited

2. Scope

a. Under the authority vested in the Commandant of the Marine Corps (CMC) by Title 10 USC, the CG, Marine Corps Combat Development Command (MCCDC) advises and guides Marine Corps commanders of the operating forces and supporting establishments in all matters related to training and education.

b. The CG, TECOM is responsible for validating training and education requirements and overseeing formal school training and education. The Ground T&R Manual Review Battle Rhythm establishes the frequency for development, review, validation and revision of all Ground T&R Manuals and Programs of Instruction within the Formal Learning Centers.

c. Tasks

(1) Advocates

(a) Partner with CG, TECOM to manage and provide content focus to the development, review, validation and revision of T&R Manual events and outcomes.

(b) Act as final adjudicator in all substantive matters.

(2) CG, TECOM

(a) Publish and manage charters for each TRMG.

(b) Partner with appropriate advocate to host, manage and provide process focus to development, review, validation and revision of T&R Manual events and outcomes.

(c) Act as final adjudicator in all matters pertaining to T&R Manual administrative format, standards development and training venue regarding "core plus" events to be conducted either in a Formal, Managed on the Job Training (MOJT) or Distance Learning (DL) setting.

(d) Assign, as appropriate, learning center representatives from both Training Command and Education Command (resident and non-resident), to support TRMG Charter Terms of Reference and community of charter groups.

(e) Establish a TRMG Battle Rhythm that supports TRMG Charter Terms of Reference and the community of charter groups.

(3) Commanders, Marine Corps Forces

(a) Assign Subject Matter Experts (SME) from appropriate occupational fields/communities to support TRMG Charter Terms of Reference and community of charter groups.

(b) Provide content focus to the development, review, validation and revision of T&R Manual events and outcomes.

3. <u>Information</u>. TECOM, Ground Training Division (C 469), maintains staff cognizance over all TRMG charters including hosting, chairing and facilitation all T&R conferences and training standards reviews conducted by TRMGs. Submit all recommendations concerning TRMG Charter framework to CG, TECOM via Operations Branch, Ground Training Division (C 469OPS).

4. <u>Command</u>. This Manual is applicable to the Marine Corps Total Force.

5. <u>Certification</u>. Reviewed and approved this date.

GEORGE J. FLYNN
Deputy Commandant for
Combat Development and Integration

Distribution: PCN 10031982600

   Copy to: 7000260 (2)
             8145001 (1)

3

LOCATOR SHEET

Subj: TRAINING AND READINESS MANUAL GROUP (TRMG) CHARTER TERMS OF REFERENCE

Location: _____
(Indicate location(s) of copy(ies) of this Order.)

RECORD OF CHANGES

Log completed change action as indicated.

Change Number	Date of Change	Date Entered	Signature of Person Incorporated Change

TRMG CHARTER TERMS

TABLE OF CONTENTS

TRMG CHARTER TERMS

CHAPTER 1

MISSION ESSENTIAL TASK LIST (METL)

CHAPTER 1

MISSION ESSENTIAL TASK LIST (METL)

1. <u>Mission Essential Task List (METL)</u>. The METL is the commander's tool for remaining focused on mission accomplishment and contains the list of a command's essential tasks with appropriate conditions and performance standards to ensure successful mission accomplishment. MCWP 5-1 (Marine Corps Planning Process), MCRP 3-0A, and the Joint Training Manual (CJCSM 3500.03) describe the Mission Analysis and METL development process. METLs are derived from essential tasks and the application of standards of performance required to accomplish them.

(a) A Combatant Commander's (COCOM) Joint Mission Essential Task List (JMETL) draws on the Universal Joint Task List (UJTL) task library and lists the tasks, conditions and standards that the COCOM identifies as required assigned missions. Marine Forces commanders employ a similarly disciplined process to review their mission assignments in Operation Plans, Concept Plan, Operation Orders, and other JMETLs and METLs from higher or adjacent units. A commander's mission analysis should capture first -- in language which is locally understood -- what the mission essential tasks are and then employ the Marine Corps Task List (MCTL) to translate those tasks into universal understanding. If the task library requires a new task, the commander nominates one through appropriate chain of command for incorporation into the MCTL. The METL framework includes "conditions" that may affect task performance, and the "standards" to which the tasks must be performed. A METL is a comprehensive command and mission specific list of a unit's Mission Essential Tasks (METs).

(b) Prior to convening of the TRMG T&R development and maintenance cycle, the Advocate will be responsible for Core METL validation. The recommended METL will be forwarded to Deputy Commandant CD&I per MCO 3500.110.

2. <u>Ground Training and Readiness (T&R) Program</u>. The Ground T&R Program serves as a single reference for ground occupational field, individual and collective training and is maintained by CG, TECOM (C 469). The program is designed to maintain up-to-date standards to meet operational needs set forth by the approved Core METs. In order to support this, the T&R Manual review and validation process will be conducted systematically per a service level battle rhythm coordinated and published annually by CG, TECOM (C 469).

CHAPTER 2

ROLES AND RESPONSIBILITIES

TRMG CHARTER TERMS

CHAPTER 2

ROLES AND RESPONSIBILITIES

1. <u>Overarching Concept</u>. The following tenets are provided as guidance to each TRMG charter group.

   a. The main effort of each TRMG charter group is to validate tasks contained within each respective T&R Manual, ensuring compliance with Marine Corps policies contained in the following documents: MCO 1200.13F (Marine Corps Front End Analysis Program), MCO P3500.72A (Ground T&R Program), NAVMC 1553.1 (Marine Corps Systems Approach to Training User's Guide) MCO 1553.3 (Unit readiness Planning Program).

   b. Meeting Schedule. The T&R Conference Battle Rhythm will be published annually via MARADMIN, and will be available via the TECOM website listed under the Ground Training Division (C 469), Operations Branch. The Battle Rhythm will indicate TRMG meeting frequency for the current fiscal year and forecasted frequency for the following fiscal year. Members will participate in additional video teleconferences and meetings as required by the TRMG Chair. TRMG members will be notified of additional meetings by the TRMG Chair via Naval Message followed by e-mail requesting confirmation of attendance.

   c. Revisions Approval. Following appropriate staffing, the TRMG Chair will submit the validated, Advocate-adjudicated draft T&R Manual revision to CG, TECOM for approval and signature.

   d. Marine Corps Training Information Management System (MCTIMS) Input. All initial T&R Manual revisions will be entered into MCTIMS. Upon CG, TECOM approval of T&R Manuals, MCTIMS will be updated by Ground Training Division (C 469) to reflect approved revisions.

2. <u>CG TECOM, Ground Training Division (C 469)</u>

   a. Maintain staff cognizance over Ground T&R program, all TRMG charters and host, chair and facilitate all T&R conferences and training standards reviews conducted by TRMGs.

   b. Coordinate the development and maintenance of all TRMG charters to ensure consistency of expectations and process followed by all TRMGs.

3. <u>TRMG Chair</u>

   a. The TRMG Chair is the designated HQ, TECOM representative, responsible to CG, TECOM and the Advocate, listed in appendix D, for the products the team is chartered to accomplish.

   b. The TRMG Chair in coordination with the Advocate will collect and present significant training issues/concerns to the TRMG for consideration.

c. The TRMG Chair is required to conduct all pre-conference and post-conference actions in accordance with the TRMG Chair Confirmation Checklist (Appendix B).

d. The TRMG Chair will ensure that funding for travel and per diem of all TRMG charter members is included in Defense Travel System (DTS). All other personnel requiring attendance to TRMG charter conferences must contact the TRMG Chair for space availability members and invitees. If the conference location is at capacity, the TRMG Chair will restrict conference attendance.

e. The TRMG Chair will ensure access to MCTIMS is granted to TRMG members as required to support the conference. Following the conference, the TRMG Chair will revoke MCTIMS access as appropriate.

f. CG, TECOM (C 469) maintains both administrative and substantive authority over the following T&R Manuals: MCCS Vols I and II, T3 and TMOS. Prior to commencement of these T&R Conferences, CG, TECOM (C 469) will internally designate an appropriate individual to provide substantive adjudication as required. The respective Task Analyst will remain the conference "Chair".

4. Occupational Field Advocate Representative

a. Prior to commencement of TRMG validate Core METLs, per MCO 3500.110.

b. Adjudicate all substantive T&R issues.

5. TRMG Charter Members. Subject Matter Experts (SME) assigned to the TRMG will be required to:

a. Respond to TRMG Chair correspondence in a timely fashion (five working days).

b. Attend TRMG conferences. If the designated charter representative cannot attend a scheduled conference, an alternate with the same authority to speak for and/or vote on issues will be assigned to take his/her place.

c. Review the reference and the current version of the T&R Manual.

d. Discuss and make recommendations on issues brought before TRMG.

e. Complete tasks as established by the TRMG Chair.

f. Focus on Individual Core/Core Plus (events) and Collective (events) that support Core METs and/or MCTLs.

g. Recommend realistic sustainment training intervals to maintain minimal proficiency and capability required for all tasks.

h. Recommend venue to conduct individual core training (Formal, MOJT or DL).

i. Identify support requirements, both external and internal, required for Marines to complete an event. All ordnance classifications (DODIC) are required to be listed by required quantities.

j. Coordinate with the TRMG Chair for all issues/concerns regarding the T&R Manual.

k. Complete conference TAD requests ten working days prior to the T&R conference start date, utilizing the SME TAD Request Form (Appendix C-1).

l. Provide support for the entering of data within MCTIMS.

m. Provide learning analysis data for newly created events to the FLCs.

n. Recommend readiness policy development and improvements.

o. Provide Subject Matter Expert (SME) support to other TRMGs as requested, by the TRMG Chair or the Advocate.

p. Provide recommendations for the use of simulations and/or distance learning products to supplement or replace live training as appropriate.

TRMG CHARTER TERMS

CHAPTER 3

PRE-CONFERENCE ACTIONS

CHAPTER 3

PRE-CONFERENCE ACTIONS

1. Major Pre-Conference Actions

    a. Conduct of Front End Analysis.

    b. Identification of Subject Matter Expertise (SME).

    c. Designation of TRMG members.

2. Front End Analysis (FEA). The FEA Program provides extensive, high quality management job performance information for the development of individual training standards, and the validation of Occupational Field structure based upon Marine Corps needs.

    a. FEA studies are initiated on a regularly scheduled basis, or with:

        (1) Introduction of new or better weapons/equipment systems requiring new operator/maintainer tasks;

        (2) Organizational changes, i.e., changes in MOS structure, force structure, and career field realignments;

        (3) Doctrinal changes required by new laws, Department of Defense requirements, and Marine Corps needs;

        (4) Evaluations indicating that a performance/training deficiency exists;

        (5) Recommendation from higher headquarters; and/or

        (6) Special requests.

    b. FEA Process. The FEA process model is four months in duration. Initial study preparation is conducted by the TECOM GTD Task Analysts along with the Advocate in order to scope objectives. Prior to the T&R Conference, the TRMG will be provided completed FEA data for their respective communities, which will be utilized at the T&R Conference to develop training requirements.

3. Identification of SME Support Requirements

    a. SME requirements will be identified six months prior to conference commencement.

    b. Three months prior to conference commencement, CG, TECOM will release a conference message containing web link with read-ahead information. Attendees are expected to be familiar with MCO P3500.72_ and their respective T&R Manual prior to commencement of conferences.

4. <u>Membership Assignment</u>. Designated commands and members of the TRMG are listed in Appendix A. Membership is segregated into voting and non-voting members, including designated MOS Advocate adjudicators.

a. CG, TECOM, in coordination with TRMG, will appoint designated TRMG charter member representatives in writing. Each TRMG charter will be tailored to its respective community prior to conference commencement in accordance with Appendix A of this directive.

b. TRMG Charter Member Representatives:

(1) Authority to speak for the representative command/DC, or agency.

(2) Authority to vote on substantive issues.

(3) Military rank of Staff Sergeant or higher (CWO3-CWO5 and Major or above for collective events above level 6000).

(4) General Schedule (GS) grade of 11 or higher.

(5) Primary membership is restricted to Subject Matter Experts (SME) for the respective T&R community Manual.

CHAPTER 4

CONDUCT OF CONFERENCE

TRMG CHARTER TERMS

CHAPTER 4

CONDUCT OF CONFERENCE

1. Major Conference Agenda Items

    a. Introduction/remarks

    b. FEA brief

    c. T&R Manual Brief

    d. Validation of individual and collective events

    e. Validation of training venue

    f. Adjudication of substantive issues requiring a vote

    g. Adjudication of training venue issues requiring a vote

    h. Decision to authorize Formal Learning Centers to begin the learning analysis process for new events

    i. Entering of T&R data into MCTIMS

2. Adjudication Procedures. The adjudicator will be the Advocate's representative. The representative must be the grade of Maj or above. The Adjudicator must be present during the conference or available to discuss issues telephonically or via VTC. Adjudicators (Appendix A-1) will be identified to conferees prior to the discussion of any TRMG issues.

    a. The goal of the TRMG is to achieve consensus for all standards issues. All items recommended for inclusion and deletion to the T&R Manual securing a TRMG consensus will be included in the final staffing draft. If recommendations cannot achieve consensus they will be brought to the floor for resolution with a vote. All major command representatives in the TRMG who are charter members will have one vote. Neither the TRMG Chair, nor any other TECOM HQ representatives will have a vote on substantive issues however; the exception is per chapter 2 paragraph 3.f of this manual. However, on issues concerning T&R Manual administrative format, standards development and training venue regarding "core plus" events to be conducted either in a formal or Managed On the Job Training (MOJT) setting. The TRMG Chair or HQ TECOM representative at the grade of Maj or above will be the adjudication authority.

    b. For each contentious issue requiring a vote, one representative from the majority and one representative from the minority, each appointed by the TRMG Chair, will produce a summary of their respective positions. A report addressing all dissenting opinions will be included in the Record of Proceedings (ROP). In the case of a tie, the Adjudicator will decide what will be included in the final draft document. Voting will be conducted by a show of hands with the majority position included in the draft T&R Manual.

    c. In the event that the occupational community has more than one designated FLC and/or detachment, CG TECOM will designate which representative will cast a deciding vote for all FLCs.

    d. The TRMG Chair will decide whether an issue is substantive or not before voting occurs.

CHAPTER 5

POST CONFERENCE ACTIONS

TRMG CHARTER TERMS

CHAPTER 5

POST CONFERENCE ACTIONS

1. Major Post-Conference Actions

    a. TRMG Chair completes and publish conference Record of Proceedings via naval message format.

    b. Commences T&R Manual staffing for approval.

2. Record of Proceedings (ROP). The results of the TRMG conference will be captured in the ROP and consist of the following information:

    a. List of attendees

    b. List of additions and deletions.

    c. Dissenting opinions report for all contentious issues.

    d. Recapitulation of adjudicated issues.

    e. Explicit direction to the FLC authorizing or disapproving commencement of learning analysis of individual events in order to develop or modify a POI.

    f. POA&M for staffing, signature and POI submission.

    g. The ROP will indicate that TRMG members validated the pertinent task list(s), considered agenda items developed from IRFs, AIRS, EOCC, and surveys, and sought and considered MCCLL information pertinent to the course being reviewed by the board.

    h. The TRMG Chair will ensure that upon completion of the T&R conference that the ROP is finalized, signed by all members, and is provided for review to the Head, GTD for review at the T&R conference hot wash.

3. T&R Manual Staffing. The goal is to obtain CG, TECOM signature approving the T&R Manual within 130 days of adjourning the T&R Conference. The TRMG Chair will produce a final draft for staffing on the GTD Website within 60 days of the conclusion of the T&R Conference. The final draft will remain on the website for 30 days. Included at the link for the document will be a Staffing Comments Matrix and the ROP.

    a. The TRMG Chair will draft a Naval Message for release once the final draft document is posted on the GTD website directing all commands represented at the TRMG to read the draft T&R Manual and the ROP and provide comments via the Comment Matrix. Commands will compile all comments and forward comments to GTD via the GTD Operations organizational mailbox: TECOM.GTB.OPS@usmc.mil.

b. The TRMG Chair will characterize all comments returned by reviewers of the T&R Manual in one of four ways:

(1) Substantive, requiring formal adjudication.

(2) Substantive, but previously answered during conference.

(3) Administrative, requiring correction by the Task Analyst.

(4) Procedural, related to business rules of conference or staffing, requiring response by the TRMG Chair.

c. Comments requiring adjudication:

(1) The TRMG Chair will prepare a decision paper for those staffing comments requiring adjudication by the conference adjudicator. The adjudicator will have the following choices, depending on the type of substantive comment:

(2) For recommended additions:

(a) "Disapproved." (All items must have justification, no matter how concise).

(b) "Approved." Additions approved by the adjudicator will be will be emailed to all voting members of the TRMG along with the original staffing comments.

(3) For recommended deletions:

(a) "Disapproved." (discussion optional).

(b) "Approved." Deletions approved by the adjudicator will be emailed to all voting members of the TRMG along with the original staffing comments.

(4) All staffing documents will be summarized in the Executive Summary of the T&R Manual signature package. All staffing documents and the final signature draft will be posted at the same link as the final staffing draft until the formally signed NAVMC order is posted by Headquarters Marine Corps (ARDB) http://www.marines.mil/news/publications/Pages/Orders.aspx.

4. Formal Learning Centers (FLCs). All FLCs affected by changes to the T&R Manual will be provided documentation for modified, changed and/or newly created tasks.

TRMG CHARTER TERMS

APPENDIX A

TRMG MEMBERSHIP

COMMAND	REPRESENTATIVE(S)	POSITION	STATUS	ROLE / RESPONSIBILITY	DSN
CG TECOM	Director, Ground Training Division	T&R Chair	Voting	T&R Oversight	XXX- XXXX
D/C HQMC PP&O	Occupational Field Advocates	T&R Adjudicator	Voting	Operational Oversight	XXX- XXXX
D/C HQMC I&L	Occupational Field Advocates	T&R Adjudicator	Voting	Operational Oversight	XXX- XXXX
Chaplain of the Marine Corps	Occupational Field Advocates	T&R Adjudicator	Voting	Operational Oversight	XXX- XXXX
Director Health & Services	Occupational Field Advocates	T&R Adjudicator	Voting	Operational Oversight	XXX- XXXX
Director C4	Occupational Field Advocates	T&R Adjudicator	Voting	Operational Oversight	XXX- XXXX
Director Public Affairs	Occupational Field Advocates	T&R Adjudicator	Voting	Operational Oversight	XXX- XXXX
Director Intelligence, HQMC	Occupational Field Advocates	T&R Adjudicator	Voting	Operational Oversight	XXX- XXXX
Staff Judge Advocate to the Commandant	Occupational Field Advocates	T&R Adjudicator	Voting	Operational Oversight	XXX- XXXX
D/C Manpower and Reserve Affairs	Occupational Field Advocates	T&R Adjudicator	Voting	Operational Oversight	XXX- XXXX
CG Marine Corps Recruiting Command	Occupational Field Advocates	T&R Adjudicator	Voting	Operational Oversight	XXX- XXXX
Director Marine Corps Information Operations Center	Occupational Field Advocates	T&R Adjudicator	Voting	Operational Oversight	XXX- XXXX
Director Marine Corps Safety Division	Occupational Field Advocates	T&R Adjudicator	Voting	Operational Oversight	XXX- XXXX
COMARFORCOM	OPFOR	Member	Voting	Operating Forces issues	XXX- XXXX
COMARFORPAC	OPFOR	Member	Voting	Operating Forces issues	XXX- XXXX
COMARFORRES	OPFOR	Member	Voting	Reserve component issues	XXX- XXXX
CG I MEF	OPFOR	Member	Voting	Operating Forces issues	XXX- XXXX
CG II MEF	OPFOR	Member	Voting	Operating Forces issues	XXX- XXXX
CG III MEF	OPFOR	Member	Voting	Operating Forces issues	XXX- XXXX
CG MCI EAST	OPFOR	Member	Voting	Marine Corps Base Issues	XXX- XXXX
CG MCI WEST	OPFOR	Member	Voting	Marine Corps Base Issues	XXX- XXXX
Formal Learning Centers (FLC) and or Detachments	Instructional Learning Centers	Member	Voting	Curriculum Oversight	N/A

Enclosure (1)

TRMG CHARTER TERMS

APPENDIX B

TRMG Chair Confirmation Checklist

TRMG CHAIR: (Name)			
T&R MANUAL: (T&R Manual Name)			
PRE-CONFERENCE ACTIONS			
Mission Essential Tasks (MET)	**Y**	**N**	**N/A**
T&R Manual contains METs			
METs verified within the Marine Corps Task List (MCTL)			
Front End Analysis (FEA)			
FEA survey completed Date:			
Coordination with TDB has been conducted identifying a briefer for the T&R Manual conference: **Briefer Name**			
Occupational Field Sponsor (OccFld Sponsor)			
Coordination with the OccFld Advocate has been conducted, identifying conference Battle Rhythm schedule and identification of Subject Matter Experts, required to attend the T&R Manual conference			
Occupational Sponsor attending conference: **OccFld Advocate Rank, Name**			
Automated Message Handling System (AMHS)			
T&R Manual Conference announcement message released (containing conference read ahead information and instructions) MSG# _____			
Conference Location			
Coordination with GTD Operations has been completed, identifying the conference location			
Location room numbers # _____			
Location address: _____			
SME, TAD Request Forms			
Coordination with GTD Operations has been conducted in order to e-mail travel forms to SMEs and follow up with completion and turn in of travel requirements			
Line of Accounting is attached to all SME orders Qty Funded			
_____ Qty of SMEs attending conference ___ I MEF, ___ II MEF, ___ III MEF, _____ MARFORRES, _____ MARFORPAC, _____ FLC (Ensure that the list of attendees is attached to the checklist)			
SME Lodging			
Quantico lodging (Liversedge) contacted in order to lock on a block of rooms			
Confirmation number for Liversedge (blocked off rooms) # _____			
Audio/Visual Equipment			
Any deficiency for audio/video equipment has been identified to GTD operations			
___ Qty of projectors required ___ Qty of laptops required ___ Qty of projection screens required			
Conference Binders/Folders			
All binders and folders assembled, containing conference related data burned to compact discs			
Marine Corps Training Information Management System (MCTIMS)			
Accessibility to MCTIMS has been obtained for SMEs that will enter data			
T&R Manual Brief			

Coordination with GTD Operations has been conducted for Ops T&R brief scheduling: **Briefer Name**			

CONDUCT OF CONFERENCE			
Conference Business Rules			
Conference attendees identified (per the charter), all unauthorized personnel dismissed per the directive			
Introductory remarks conducted by T&R Manual Section Head (Branch Head as required)			
FEA brief conducted by the Training Development Branch			
T&R brief conducted by the Operations Branch			
All individual and collective events validated			
Formal Learning Center briefed as to whether or not they are authorized to pull events to begin the learning analysis process for newly created events			
Adjudicators have been identified to conference attendees, of who will be the approving authority for additions/changes and or deletion of T&R tasks prior to CG TECOM, T&R Manual signature			

POST CONFERENCE ACTIONS			
Hot Wash			
Records of Proceedings (ROP) completed			
All data inputted within MCTIMS (upon completion of conference), if not what is the current percentage completed %			
Draft message completed for T&R 30 day review			

TRMG CHARTER TERMS

APPENDIX C

SME TAD Request Form

SME FUNDING REQUEST

NAME OF TRAVELER:		RANK/ TITLE:		SUBJECT MATTER EXPERT Yes ☐ No ☐

MOS:		FULL SSN:		UNIT ADDRESS:	

PHONE:
- COMM:
- DSN:
- FAX:

EMAIL ADDRESS:

CONFERENCE TITTLE:

CONFERENCE LOCATION:

DEPARTURE DATE		RETURN DATE		# OF DAYS TAD	

MODE OF TRAVEL

COMMERCIAL	GOVERNMENT	POV
RAIL ☐ AIR ☐ BUS ☐ RENTAL ☐	AIR ☐ VEH ☐ SHIP ☐	CONSTRUCTIVE COST ☐ ADVANTAGEOUS TO GOVT ☐

LODGING: GOV. QTRS AVAILABLE: YES ☐ NO ☐

AVAILABILITY #:

NON-AVALABILIILITY #

NOTE: IF GOVT QTRS ARE NOT AVAIL YOU MUST OBTAIN A NON-AVAIL #.

PER DIEM RATES:		OTHER EXPENSES:	
LODGING:		PARKING:	LODGING TAXES
M&IE:		CTO FEE	GAS FOR RENTAL
TOTAL:		MILEAGE TO/FR AIRPORT:	MILEAGE TO/FR TAD SITE:

RENTAL COST:		AIR FARE COST:		USE AMOUNTS FROM DRAFT DTS ORDERS
TOTAL COST BEING CLAIMING:				

REMARS:

TRMG CHARTER TERMS

APPENDIX D

Ground T&R Matrix (Including Occupational Field Advocate Representatives Offices)

NAVMC	SHORT TITLE	OCCFld SPONSOR
NAVMC 3500.59	ADVICE TRAIN & ASSIST (ATA)	HQMC PPO
NAVMC 3500.89	AMMUNITIONS	MCSC
NAVMC 3500.2A	AMPHIBIOUS ASSAULT VEHICLE	HQMC PPO
NAVMC 3500.23	ANGLICO	HQMC PPO
NAVMC 3500.7	ARTILLERY	HQMC PPO
NAVMC 3500.63	AT/CIP	HQMC PPO
NAVMC 3500.29	CBIRF	HQMC PPO
NAVMC 3500.78	CBRN (NBC)	HQMC PPO
NAVMC 3500.22	CIVIL AFFAIRS	MCCDC
NAVMC 3500.77	COMBAT CAMERA	HQMC PA
NAVMC 3500.54A	COMMAND & CONTROL (C2)	HQMC PPO
NAVMC 3500.56A	COMMUNICATIONS	HQMC C4
NAVMC 3500.25A	DISTRIBUTION MANAGEMENT (DMO)	HQMC PPO
NAVMC 3500.12A	ENGINEER & UTILITIES	HQMC I&L
NAVMC 3500.66A	EXPLOSIVE ORDNANCE DISPOSAL (EOD)	HQMC I&L
NAVMC 3500.69	FINANCIAL MANAGEMENT	HQMC P&R
NAVMC 3500.35A	FOOD SERVICES	HQMC PPO
NAVMC 3500.6A	GROUND ELECTRONICS	HQMC C4
NAVMC 3500.33A	GROUND ORDNANCE MAINTENANCE	HQMC I&L
NAVMC 3500.110	GROUND SAFETY	HQMC SD
NAVMC 3500.17A	GROUND SENSOR	HQMC PPO
NAVMC 3500.64	GROUND SUPPLY	HQMC I&L
NAVMC 3500.84	HEALTH SERVICES	HQMC TMO
NAVMC 3500.44	INFANTRY	HQMC PPO
NAVMC 3500.90	INFORMATION OPERATIONS	HQMC PPO
NAVMC 3500.100	INTELLIGENCE	HQMC I
NAVMC 3500.82	LEGAL	HQMC JAS
NAVMC 3500.16	LIGHT ARMORED RECONNAISSANCE VEHICLE	HQMC PPO
NAVMC 3500.27B	LOGISTICS	HQMC I&L
NAVMC 3500.5	MAGTF PLANNER	HQMC PPO
NAVMC 3500.18A	MARINE CORPS COMMON SKILLS (VOL 1)	TECOM TMEB
NAVMC 3500.19	MARINE CORPS COMMON SKILLS (VOL 2)	TECOM TMEB
NAVMC 3500.13A	MARINE CORPS COMMUNITY SERVICES (MCX)	HQMC MRX
NAVMC 3500.61	MARINE CORPS SECURITY FORCE REGIMENT	MCSF REG
NAVMC 3500.98	MARINE CORPS EMBASSY SECURITY GUARD	MSG
NAVMC 3500.97	MARINE SPECIAL OPERATIONS COMMAND (MARSOC)	HQMC PPO
NAVMC 3500.99	MARINE EXPEDITIONARY UNIT (MEU)	HQMC PPO
NAVMC 3500.10B	MILITARY POLICE & CORRECTIONS	HQMC PPO
NAVMC 3500.39A	MOTOR TRANSPORT	HQMC I&L
NAVMC 3500.70	MOUNTAIN WARFARE OPERATIONS	MAGTF TC
NAVMC 3500.28A	MUSIC	HQMC PA
NAVMC 3500.72	NON-LETHAL WEAPONS	HQMC I&L
NAVMC 3500.65	OPERATIONS CULTURE & LANGUAGE	HQMC I
NAVMC 3500.36A	OPERATIONS TACTICS & INSTRUCTIONS	MCTOG
NAVMC 3500.3B	PERSONNEL & ADMINISTRATION	HQMC MI
NAVMC 3500.9A	PUBLIC AFFAIRS	HQMC PA
NAVMC 3500.55A	RECONNAISSANCE	HQMC PPO
NAVMC 3500.71	RECRUITING & RETENTION	MCRC MMEA-2
NAVMC 3500.85	RELIGIOUS MINISTRY	HQMC Chaplain
NAVMC 3500.105	SIGNALS INTELLIGENCE	HQMC I
NAVMC 3500.42A	TACTICAL AIR CONTROL PARTY (TACP)	MAWTS
NAVMC 3500.1A	TANK	HQMC PPO
NAVMC 3500.37A	TRAIN THE TRAINER (T3)	TECOM TMEB
NAVMC 3500.41A	TRAINING MOS	TECOM CSB

Enclosure (1)

www.ingramcontent.com/pod-product-compliance
Lightning Source LLC
Chambersburg PA
CBHW080935290526
45795CB00007BA/2771